My Silly Book of
ABC's

Written by Susan Amerikaner
Illustrated by Judy Ziegler

SILVER PRESS

Amerikaner, Susan.
    My silly book of ABCs / by Susan Amerikaner;
illustrated by Judy Ziegler.
            p.   cm.
    Summary: Introduces the letters of the
alphabet through the antics of various animals
from Arnie Alligator to a zany zebra.
    [1. Alphabet.] I. Ziegler, Judy, ill. II. Title.
PZ7.A4997Mx 1989
[E]—dc19   89-5979
ISBN 0-671-68119-2   CIP
ISBN 0-671-68363-2 (lib. bdg.)   AC
ISBN 382-24672-1 (pbk)

Published by Silver Press, a division of
Silver Burdett Press, Inc.,
Simon & Schuster, Inc.,
Prentice Hall Bldg., Englewood Cliffs, NJ 07632.
Printed in the United States of America.

10 9 8 7 6 5 4 3 2

A Note to Parents

MY SILLY BOOKS are perfect for parents and children to share together. Each book is designed to introduce a beginning concept. Read each one first, just for fun. Encourage your child to look carefully. The illustrations contain additional details that reinforce concepts. Large, simple text encourages your preschool child to pick out words.

Now, look again–there's more to be found in the silly animal antics. Ask your child to think about what might come next. Be imaginative! Encourage your child to be creative and, most of all, have fun!

Aa

Arnie Alligator accepts an award
for his amazing apple pie.

apple

What an avalanche!

Bb

basket

Bears and beavers play basketball
with a boa for a basket.

Cc

cats

Cats in kitty cars eat corn,
cotton candy, and carrot cake.

Dd

Drats! What a downpour at the drive-in!

A dozen dinosaurs get drenched.

Ee

Eight energetic elephants exercise every day.

How exhausting!

Ff

food

Frannie Frog's favorite food is fudge.
She's too friendly to feast on flies.

Gg

goat

The greedy goat gobbles garbage –
greasy gravy, green grapes, and gum.

Hh

hockey

Henry Hedgehog has a horrible headache
whenever he plays hockey.

Ii

Is that an iguana eating an ice-cream cone inside an igloo?

Jj

jar

Jack Rabbit jumps into a jar of jelly.
Now Jack's in a jam!

Kk

kittens

The kittens make a king-size mess,
kicking ketchup onto the kitchen floor.

Ll

lobsters

Lively lobsters help the lazy lifeguard
hang laundry on the line.

Mm

mermaid

If you meet a mermaid with a mustache,
remember your manners! Don't mention it!

Nn

nose

Nellie Newt has a noodle on her nose and
a napkin around her neck.

Oo

octopus

The octopus opens oysters, eats oatmeal,
and plays in an orchestra – all at the same time!

Pp

panda

A panda plays piano in the park
while porcupines picnic and poodles prance.

Qq

queen

Will the quiet queen ever quit quilting?
That's quite a question.

Rr

raccoon

A rowdy raccoon rounds up a rainbow
at a rainy-day rodeo.

Six spiders stand on the soccer field
in their sneakers, socks, shirts, and shorts.

Tt

tub

Timmy Tiger finds a turkey in the tub
and has a temper tantrum.

Uu

umbrellas

Unicorns strum ukuleles under upside-down umbrellas.

Vv

vampire

The velvet-vested vampire sends his valentine
vegetable soup.

Ww

witch

The witch works out while she waits for her waterproof wig to come out of the wash.

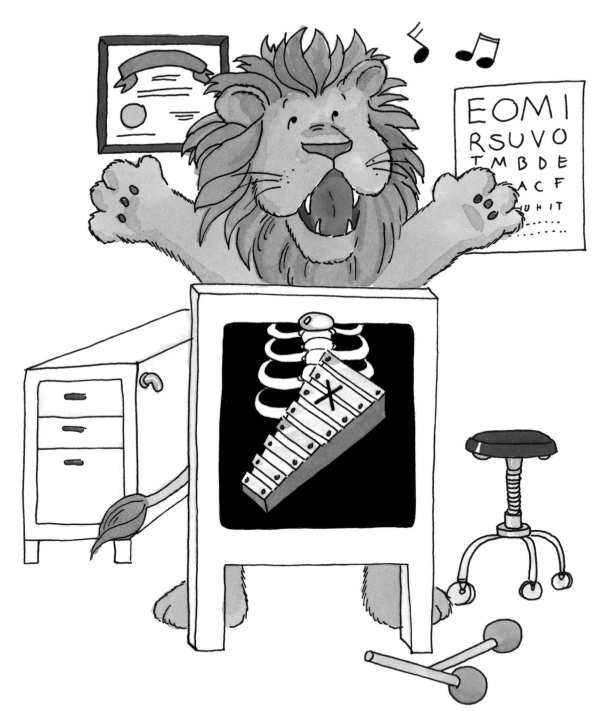

Xavier swallowed a xylophone.
X marks the spot on the x-ray.

Yy

yak

A yawning yak plays with a yo-yo
in the yard.

Zz

zebra

A zany zebra eats a zippered zucchini
at the zoo.